THE PROBLEM OF PURITY

THE
PROBLEM OF PURITY

by

VIOLET M. FIRTH

AUTHOR OF
" MACHINERY OF THE MIND," " PSYCHOLOGY
OF THE SERVANT PROBLEM," ETC.

SAMUEL WEISER
New York

Samuel Weiser, Inc.
740 Broadway
New York, N.Y. 10003

ISBN 0-87728-506-3

Printed in the U.S.A. by
Noble Offset Printers, Inc.
New York, N.Y. 10003

CONTENTS

FOREWORD

IN this book I am trying to do for my readers what I have so often done for patients who have come to me for psychotherapy. It is really a course of treatments for sex control, and the earlier chapters, which deal with standpoint and motive, should be carefully read and re-read because they are intended to produce a frame of mind in the reader, just as I would do if he or she came to me as a patient.

I do not, however, take patients now, and therefore this book must do its own work, for I cannot undertake to give interviews.

THE PROBLEM OF PURITY

I

INTRODUCTION

MANY books have been written which explain the facts of sex in simple language ; many others which make appeals for social purity ; and some few, of varying value, which deal with the problems of married life ; but, so far as I know, none have attempted to deal in a really practical manner with the difficulties of celibacy, and to follow an appeal for control of the sex instinct by practical suggestions as to the method of attaining that much-to-be-desired end.

People may be unmarried either from force of circumstances or choice. If from force of circumstances, it is exceedingly desirable that the urge of the sex instincts should not be so insistent as to cause distress, or so powerful as to place them in difficult situations. If celibacy is from choice, it is very helpful for those who make that choice to know the best way of managing their natures. There is a strategic method of approach which reduces the expenditure of repressive force to a minimum and is much more economical of energy than the frontal attack of pure will-power.

The normal desires of a man are not towards an irregular life, but rather towards the ideal woman who shall be the beloved wife, even if the ideal is no higher than physical beauty. Illicit relations are but a substitute for this ideal ; nor is it a good thing that any one should be hurried into marriage by the insistent demands of his physical nature, instead of being free to seek at his leisure for the woman who shall be his true wife, meeting his higher needs as well as his lower.

Moreover, ability to regulate the sex instinct is as necessary for happiness in married life as in single. A man must be the master of himself if he is to reach the full stature of manhood—the physical instincts which we share with the animal kingdom should not have the power to dictate to us ; we do not belong to our bodies, our bodies belong to us, to be used for the ends that reason, not emotion, shall determine. It is a tragic thing for a man to be carried along by a tide of desire while his higher self rebels at the demands of his physical needs which cannot be satisfied save by means which he feels to be degrading.

The problem of sex control is a problem for women as well as men, though not commonly in so acute a form. A girl is often ignorant of the significance of her own feelings, and owing to the sternness of the social code towards the delinquencies of her sex, she dare not dally with them ; so that her danger does not lie so much in the risks and degradations of illicit sex expression as in the discomfort and nervous disorders of undue repression.

The problem often becomes acute towards middle age, and I have known the same advice to be given to women as is sometimes

given to men, with disastrous consequences.
We should not regard a solution of the sex
problem as satisfactory which requires the
degradation of any human soul. There are
some practices which involve the degradation of another, and some which involve the
degradation of oneself ; and though, if
there must be a choice, it is better to inflict
suffering on oneself alone rather than to
involve another, the problem is not solved
by yielding to the blackmailing demands of
the lower self which, by threats of discomfort and promises of pleasure, induces
us to do what we would not do if we had
freedom of choice.

The method of sex control herein described is based on many years' experience
in dealing with sex problems in both men
and women in both clinic and private
practice. By the methods herein described
sex control can be attained and maintained
without strain or repression, even in difficult
or complicated cases of lifelong standing. It
is very much easier than it appears to be,
and the effect of the method is accumulative,

increasing in efficacy as it is persisted in. It does not produce the strain and nervousness of repression by will-power, nor does it produce sex-repulsion and incapacity for normal married life ; it is a true sublimation of the life forces, using on a higher level that which has to be denied expression on a lower level.

Did I desire to commercialise this system into a course of expensive correspondence lessons, it could no doubt be made into a profitable business, for the need for such help is much more widespread than those who have not worked along these lines would believe ; but I feel that any knowledge which can relieve human suffering should not be kept secret for the sake of profit. It is hoped that this book may be of value to the educationalist and social worker, as well as to those who have to solve problems of their own, and for this reason the chapters on the child and adolescent are added. Those who wish to teach this method of sex control to others should note carefully the method of approach employed in these pages, because it is based on experience in dealing with a wide range of cases.

First, a really vital motive for purity should be found and presented clearly to the patient ; next, specious reasonings should be dealt with so that conscience may not have a loophole ; and thirdly, a clear understanding of the facts of sex should be imparted ; this last is more important than it might appear to be, for successful sex control is impossible so long as sex is an unsolved mystery. Fourthly, each individual, whether man or woman, must be reconciled to the sex side of his or her nature, and induced to accept it as normal and wholesome, but not to treat it with familiarity or levity, as it is too often done when the taboo of silence is removed ; they should learn to regard sex, not as too unclean to be referred to indiscriminately, but as *too sacred*. It is this sacredness of sex, rather than its dangers, that should be emphasised. Fear is a two-edged weapon when used as a motive for control, for it causes things that are better dismissed from thought to haunt the mind.

In this book I deliberately avoid the consideration of the religious aspect of the problem because I hope that the followers of every path that leads to the Light may find it useful. I may say, however, that in my experience of sex problems I have found that the man or woman, or child, too, for that matter, who finds help in his or her religion has a much easier task than the one who has to go alone in his own strength.

II

OUR ATTITUDE TOWARDS SEX

THERE are three possible attitudes that can be assumed with regard to sex. On the one hand, it may be regarded as unclean, sinful, to be kept out of sight and mind, and to be tolerated in marriage only because of the physical impossibility of totally eliminating it ; on the other hand, it may be considered as natural and common-place as eating and drinking, and we may be advised to familiarise ourselves with Nature's method of continuing the race until it ceases to have the fascination of mystery and novelty.

I have seen both these methods tried, and both have serious drawbacks, and yet in each there is a foundation of truth which renders it impossible to ignore its view-point. Havelock Ellis, the great authority on sex psychology, has very justly pointed out that if the process of nourishment were surrounded with the same mystery as the process of reproduction, the problems of catering would be as dark and difficult as the problems of sex life, and people would be trying all manner of experiments in diet, some of which might be disastrous. It is because of the general ignorance of sex hygiene, and consequent secret and unguided experimentation that many of our social problems and diseases have arisen.

This cannot be disputed. Yet the universal instinct of mankind to keep sex out of sight cannot be without some foundation in practical experience, however perverted and remote from reality some of its methods may have become.

We have found by experience that anything which causes us to think of sex is very apt to stimulate sex feelings ; so that, if we do not wish at the moment to give expression to those feelings in acts, we had better keep away from anything which reminds us of them. Familiarity with sex is, unfortunately for the advocates of unrepression, like habituation to alcohol, it does not satiate, but demands larger doses. For this reason, modesty is a thing which we cannot afford to dispense with. We must avoid giving the stimulus if we do not desire the resulting reaction.

I suggest that we should deal with sex, not from the standpoint of its wickedness, nor of its commonplaceness, but of its sacredness. We should realise its tremendous potency on the mental as well as on the physical plane ; we should regard it as the direct expression of the Divine Life through the channel of our organisms ; it does not belong to us, to be used for our personal pleasure, for we are trustees for the race, and unborn generations are beneficiaries under this Divine Trust. This is the essence of sex life and the secret of right use of the sex force—*it is not ours, it belongs to the race.* The fact that it gives us pleasure in its use is incidental to its real object, and is simply a provision of Nature to secure that object.

The instinct of all mankind in all ages, from the most primitive to the most depraved, has always felt that sex force is rightly used only when it is used for racial ends ; as soon as it is used for personal gratification it is felt to be debased. Used rightly, it has a spiritual significance ; used wrongly, it becomes corruption.

No amount of argument concerning physiological necessity can get away from the fact that sex force, wrongly used, puts its mark on a man or woman. The lines round the eyes, the set of the lips, the carriage of the body, proclaim it, and intuition assesses them unerringly. Unless the sex force is sanctified by the fulfilment of its duties as well as the enjoyment of its pleasures, it puts the stamp of sensuality on the face and form.

Marriage implies not only exclusive possession, but home-making ; and the reason that unlegalised unions almost invariably fail to be permanent is because home-making, with the pleasures of hospitality and neighbourliness, is denied to them, and therefore they satisfy only a part of the nature.

People may have the right to take their lives into their own hands and do as they please in matters which concern no one but themselves, but in the sex relationship the rights and welfare of a third person have to be considered,—the possible child. To bring into the world a child for whom no home can be made, is to do that child a cruel wrong, and there is no contraceptive known to medical science which is absolutely dependable. I was present at a meeting for the discussion of contraceptives, and a leading authority stated that we have methods which give a 90 per cent safety, but none which give a 100 per cent safety, and not a single voice was raised in dissent. The only certain thing about contraceptives is their uncertainty.

The whole question of the use of contraceptives is not only a vexed one, but an open one ; and whatever may be said of their physiological advantages, or their spiritual disadvantages, there can be no question of their æsthetic offensiveness. No one would use them if they could help it. It is preferable from every point of view that the sex urge should be prevented from arising when not desired, than that means should be used to prevent the normal completion of its action when that action has already commenced.

III

MOTIVES FOR CONTROL

IT may be thought strange that it should appear necessary to discuss motives for purity, but a considerable section of modern thought, finding justification for its philosophy in the Freudian psychology, advocates self-expression in sex as a truer and more natural way of life than self-control. Upon a half-understood medical theory are based a philosophy and ethics which have an immediate bearing on conduct, health and national welfare, and therefore it may be as well to discuss the theory on which these are based.

The New Psychology, having discovered that sex lies at the bottom of many forms of nerve trouble, has declared in no uncertain terms the harmfulness of sex repression. I was in close touch with the early developments of psycho-analysis in England when it was believed that sex repression was at the root of all nerve problems, and that 'unrepression' would solve them all, as well as many other ills that society is heir to ; this theory proved unsatisfactory in practice ; there is more in sex life than physical desire, and with a great many temperaments, if physical expression is found in a form that outrages the moral and spiritual nature, a conflict is set up which is simply an aggravation of the original problem. I have seen much serious trouble ensue from taking the rash advice that is sometimes given.

In my opinion it is not repression that produces nerve trouble, but dissociation, which is a very different thing. In repression, we refuse to act upon an impulse ; in dissociation, we refuse to admit to ourselves that such impulses are a part of our nature, and thereby deceive ourselves. If we shirk facing ourselves in this way, our impulses, not being controlled by consciousness, get out of hand, and are very apt to express

themselves in indirect ways and in curious
symbolic and perverted forms, thus giving
rise to mental disease. It is the people
who refuse to face the facts of their
own natures and of life in general who
develop ' kinks,' and not the people who,
facing the facts, determine on a specific
line of conduct and adhere to it at all
costs.

The Freudian psychology teaches that
most forms of nerve trouble are due to
conflict between subconscious sex wishes
and an artificially trained conscience which
holds them down, and one way of resolving
the conflict is by getting rid of the repressive
conscious. When this is done by means of
' re-education ' after dream analysis, it
usually produces a feeling of relief and
freedom which is held to constitute a
cure ; this, however, is, as far as I have
been able to follow up the subsequent
history of cases so treated, followed by a
reaction, because the conflict has not been
settled but merely changed in form ; for

whereas, in the first state the social instinct was holding down the sex instinct, in the second state the sex instinct is holding down the social instinct, and the urge to be in harmony with our fellows is just as fundamental as the urge to reproduce our kind.

The unrepression of the sex instinct is very apt to lead to unlimited self-abuse, and the demoralisation and degeneration that that brings with it. This, in fact, is one of the prime risks of psycho-analytical treatment ; so much so, that it was a current saying at one time among those who were studying psycho-analysis that, although we could not agree with Freud that all our cases started with sex problems, they most of them ended with them ! One thing is quite certain, that psycho-analytical treatment is the last thing for a case in which sex has got out of control.

The one-sidedness of the Early Victorian attitude towards sex has led to a reaction, just as that attitude was itself a reaction from the Restoration grossness, and the truth, as usual, lies in the middle way. Nothing which can grip men's minds and consciences can be altogether without foundation in truth, and because we have to dissent from a doctrine or system as a whole we should not be blind to its truth in parts. The Freudian doctrine is not so much untrue as disproportionate ; the sex forces, when healthy, bear about the same proportion to life as a whole as the sex organs do to the body as a whole, it is only when something is amiss with them that they bulk unduly large in consciousness.

This instinct, however, having a very large mental aspect, is almost invariably affected when nervous trouble sets in, and therefore it is generally found to be morbid when a nerve case is psycho-analysed ; but then a morbid digestive system is just as common in neurotics and no one has yet suggested indigestion as the sole cause of mental trouble !

Sex is a subject which is very apt to obsess the minds of those who study it ; the investigator of sex psychology should be as careful in his precautions as the investigator of radio-active substances, for he is very liable to be affected by the material with which he has to work, this is not sufficiently realised by those who undertake these studies and therefore their work is apt to be biased by the warping of their own natures under the influence of the mental atmosphere in which they spend their days.

It is never wise to read books on sex, even those that plead for purity, when fatigued ; neither is it wise to read them for too long at a time, nor too many of them in rapid succession. The scientific worker in these subjects takes his risks and takes his precautions, but for the layman the advice which the caterpillar gave to Alice in Wonderland regarding the puppy-dog is the wisest : ' You let it alone, and it will let you alone.'

When the problem presents itself to consciousness it should be faced honestly and courageously and a line of conduct decided upon, and then the subject should be put aside. To be continually dwelling upon it is to induce the very condition which it is supposed to be desired to avoid. I say 'supposed' advisedly, for I have known even the best and sanest books on sex hygiene to be read from morbid motives.

As to the physiological results of continence, the new work on the ductless glands shows that the important contribution which the sex organs make to the well-being of the body is due to the interstitial cells, or framework of the organs, and not to the vital secretions themselves. These secretions represent a tremendous output of energy, and if the body has accumulated more energy than it can use, and so has become congested with the surplus, it gives a sense of relief if that surplus be disposed of in this way ; but it is not the only use that can be made of it ; it is, in fact, a very wasteful way to dispose of it, for when turned into mental channels, this energy becomes potentially creative, and has an enormous effect on vitality and capacity. The teaching on the subject of sex which is handed on from one generation of youth to another declares that sex experience is necessary to health and the development of true manliness, but it should be noted that it is not the fine, upstanding athlete whose sex desires are strongest, but rather the weakly and unwholesome-looking lad of morbid temperament, and sedentary habits.

The commencement of sex activity and the slowing down of growth take place simultaneously, for the simple reason that the life-force is being diverted from one channel into another. This does not mean that celibates become giants, because growth is limited by other means than this, but it *does* mean that if sex expression begins before maturity is reached, growth will be stunted owing to the deflection of life energy from the upbuilding of the body into the intensely vital secretions of the reproductive organs, whether that deflection be caused by actual intercourse or self-abuse. For this reason animal breeders separate the sexes as early as possible in order to prevent the premature sex activity which spoils development.

It is quite true, however, that the time of the development of the sex activities is a difficult time, and always must be so because it is a transition phase, and also because the knowledge that enables a child to understand his or her own nature is often so unwisely withheld. The method of sex control advocated in these pages will be found especially applicable to the problems of the adolescent, as it is at that period that sex control can be most readily acquired and is most needed in order to safeguard the developing life through the perils of the entry upon the experiences of adult freedom. If the perils of youth are to be avoided and a happy marriage made, it is extremely desirable that the passions should not have a casting vote in any decision.

The sex relationship between a man and a woman is very much more than physical, it is emotional, intellectual and spiritual, in so far as those aspects of the nature are developed in any given pair ; and if the intellectual and spiritual nature be active in one of the two and absent in the other, the companionship is incomplete and unsatisfying.

IV

THE PURPOSE OF THE SEX INSTINCT

IN order to handle the sex forces within ourselves we need to have a clear understanding of their nature, and not only of their physical aspect, but of their mental aspect as well, for mind and body interact, and the imagination plays a part in the sex life as well as the ductless glands.

It is also necessary to start with certain basic concepts, if any satisfactory line of action is to be arrived at. These concepts, though philosophical in their nature, are extremely practical in their effects, because they determine the attitude we assume towards sex, and attitude is all-important in this matter.

Let us ask ourselves, first of all, what Nature is aiming at, because this is the basis from which all action must start ;

there is no other. Or, if you wish to go further back in the line of causation, you may ask : What is God aiming at through Nature ? We see that Nature works, not by means of individuals, but by means of species, it is not until life has reached a very high degree of development that the individual begins to have importance.

We may conceive of Life as flowing out into manifestation through the channels of millions upon millions of individual organisms. This Life, pressing for expression through us, appears to us as the great fundamental instincts, and the chief thing we have to realise in regard to these instincts is that Nature has *adapted them to serve racial rather than personal ends*. This is a fundamental concept, and forms the basis of all attempts to control the instincts. Even the self-preservation instinct aims primarily at the preservation of the race, and preserves the individual simply as a means to that end. That is why people cling to life under conditions in which pure reason might say they were better dead ; and also why we deny to individuals the right to injure themselves with degrading drugs like opium, for the race preserves itself in the persons of the many individuals who compose it.

And likewise with the reproductive instinct, Nature aims at the continuance of the race, not at giving pleasure to individuals ; but because the achievement of any instinctive end is pleasurable, and the reproductive instinct operates at high pressure, the achievement of its end is more intensely pleasurable than the mere maintenance of life to which the self-preservation instinct prompts us. But were we to achieve the maintenance of life only by means of a great effort, the pleasure of the satisfaction of that instinct would be as great as the pleasure of the satisfaction of the reproductive instinct. Who can doubt that the traveller who escapes from the wolves, or the sailor who is saved from a shipwreck, experiences a profound satisfaction ?

Let us therefore realise that the pleasure we experience in the satisfaction of an instinct is incidental to Nature's purpose,

and does not conſtitute the reason for the
exiſtence of that inſtinct. The capacity to
derive pleasure from the use of an inſtinct is
implanted in our natures because it is the
simpleſt and moſt effective way of inducing
us to make use of those faculties with which
the inſtinct is concerned. If we try and
think of the *purpose* of an inſtinct as apart
from the pleasure its exercise can give, we
shall get a truer concept of it, and have
gone much further towards its right management than we shall do if we only think of
our personal needs and desires in relation
to it.

Let us, then, make up our minds to this,
that the sex force within us does not belong
to us, it belongs to the race, and we are
only truſtees for it, and that if we use it for
personal ends such as physical pleasure, it
is as if we were misappropriating truſt
money. The beneficiary under the truſt is
the race that is to be, the nation of the
future, and whenever we think of our
personal needs and desires in regard to sex,
let us also think of the unborn child to

which the gratification of those needs might give life, and for whom there can be no home.

Whenever the sex needs make themselves felt, let us remind ourselves that we are feeling within us the pressure of the Divine Life ; let us regard it as the most sacred thing that God has entrusted to us, and let us make up our minds to keep it scrupulously clean, pure and holy.

V

THE STRATEGY OF SEX CONTROL

MOST people, when they try to control the sex impulse, do it by sheer will-power, but there is a much easier way than this ; and although will-power cannot be dispensed with, there is a way of using it, a ſtrategical method of attack, which makes the task infinitely easier.

In addition to the physical machinery by means of which Nature carries on the life of the race, there are the nerve-controls which operate it, and these are juſt as important and not nearly so well under-ſtood ; but for the purpose of this book it is all-important that their nature should be thoroughly grasped, because it is by manipulating them by means of the picture-images of the imagination that the control of the sex forces is obtained.

Supposing the idea of sex arises in the consciousness, certain physiological changes in the sex organs immediately take place, because the mental image of the sex-idea is telegraphed along the nerves that lead to these organs, and they immediately prepare themselves for action. Between times they are quiescent. The first change which takes place is an increased blood supply to the parts concerned by means of just the same mechanism as that which produces blushing of the face in response to an idea.

If the stimulus be withdrawn immediately by, say, the attention being distracted, the extra blood re-enters the circulation and the veins of the reproductive organs return to their normal state ; but if the stimulus be continued, then the blood pressure in the organs causes the cycle of sex activity to run its course.

Let it be clearly understood that the secretion of the seminal fluid does not resemble the secretion of urine by the kidneys, which is made drop by drop and stored in the bladder for periodical discharge. This is a mistaken analogy which has misled so many, who think that, because sex desire is strong, the seminal fluid must have accumulated within them and that discharge is imperative. Whereas the seminal fluid is only secreted *after* the organs become engorged with blood as the result of a nerve impulse. It therefore follows that if the nerve impulse can be controlled, and prevented from increasing the blood supply to the organs, the seminal fluid will not be secreted.

Sex desire is caused by the pressure of extra *blood* in the organs, not by pressure of accumulated seminal fluid, which is proved by the fact that desire may come up and die away repeatedly without any secretion being formed, and that sex desire is present in the female as well as the male, that it continues after the glands have lost their power of secretion owing to old age, and that if the reproductive organs are removed after the age of puberty, the emotional aspect of sex desire is unaffected.

Our problem, then, is to control the

original impulse which sent the blood to the organs, so let us study its workings.

This impulse has a circular motion, an outgoing impulse from the brain to the organs causing them to react, and a return impulse from the organs to the brain which causes the sensation to be felt. A sexual image in the imagination will send an impulse along the outgoing nerves, but equally, any stimulation of the reproductive organs will cause sensation to be sent back to the brain, where it will give rise to a sexual image ; the impulse may start at either end of the circuit, either in an idea in the imagination, or in a sensation in the organs themselves ; the idea gives rise to the sensation, and the sensation to the idea, and the impulse is telegraphed round and round the nerve circuit several times, gaining strength as it goes, till it finally results in the explosion of energy which forms the orgasm : therefore the secret of stopping undesired sex reactions is to break this circuit.

First of all, let all external stimulation of

the organs, whether accidental or deliberate, be carefully avoided ; unless this be done, the impulse will continually be restarted on its circuit, however often that circuit may be broken by the mind. Tight clothing is a common cause of stimulation, especially in growing children, and is often the starting-point of bad habits ; and to leave a baby too long without attention is simply asking for trouble. Being too warm in bed, and having the bladder over-full, especially when in bed, are also causes of stimulation ; meat is also a stimulant to a certain extent, and alcohol is the most potent sex-stimulant of all. These factors should all be dealt with first in order to clear the ground for the mental control of the sex force and place no unnecessary difficulties in the way.

The sex image may arise spontaneously or be caused by something read, heard, or seen. If people persist in reading un-wholesome books and looking at unpleasant pictures, they will not be able to control the sex forces, because they are constantly ſtimulating them. If they are obliged to associate with people who indulge in talk and innuendo on sex ſubjeᶜts, their task will naturally be more difficult than if they were with more wholesome companions, but they can at leaſt refrain from contributing their quota to the conversational mud. The method of thought control which I will explain, will prevent impure suggeſtions from entering the mind and gaining a foothold there.

People who have sex problems to solve generally have some mental piᶜture or set of ideas which gives rise to the desire, and this especially applies to those who indulge in self-abuse ; they invariably make use of phantasy. These mental piᶜtures rise in consciousness with extraordinary vividness and cause ſtrong sex desire. If the will is used to drive away these piᶜtures, it merely focuses the attention on them, and however much the attention be turned away from them, they seem merely to be waiting their opportunity to spring up again. A direᶜt attack by the will often defeats its own ends, but WHAT THE IMAGINATION HAS MADE, THE IMAGINATION CAN BREAK.

Look right at the sensual image, visualise it clearly, and then imagine it to explode into a thousand fragments. Now in its place deliberately picture with all the clearness you possibly can, a mental image, symbolic of purity. See a tall white lily or a fruit tree in blossom, or a favourite picture of an inspiring theme. Smash the ugly image and replace it with a beautiful one, that is the secret of dealing with undesirable mental pictures.

When an image has once been smashed in this way, it will be the pale ghost of its former self on its next appearance, and after it has been dealt with a few times, it will be gone for good. True, others may appear until the physical conditions settle down, but they can be dealt with in the same way as their predecessors till all are overcome, and habits of purity built up which become just as fixed as habits of self-indulgence. It is because habits that are not used soon fade and are forgotten, and actions that are persisted in soon become habits, that we can do so much for ourselves by mind-training.

If evil dreams trouble the sleep, the imagination can again be used for protection. Visualise oneself as sleeping on an island set in a silver sea across which no impurity can come, or visualise guardian angels at the head and foot of the bed, into whose presence no evil dare venture ; or if the temptations of the abyss be so strong that they almost seem to be external to oneself, imagine a great mailed archangel like St. Michael drawing a flaming circle of pro-tection round the bed with a fiery sword, and himself standing on guard all night while you sleep secure with that magic circle ; and then imagine a white cross lying on your breast so that you yourself may not pollute that circle by evil thoughts arising in sleep. Always fight the imagina-tion with the imagination by exchanging one image for another.

VI

THE CONTROL OF THE SEX FORCE

IN the previous chapters the control of
the mental half of the circuit of sex
impulse was shown : in this chapter we
will deal with the method of controlling the
physical half of that circuit.

It muſt be clearly realised, however, that
after the sex reactions have proceeded a
certain way, they will go on to their natural
conclusion ; the time at which to ſtop them
is when the firſt rush of blood to the organs
makes itself felt. To dally with the sensations until orgasm is beginning is very
undesirable and apt to cause nervous tension.
If, however, the following syſtem of thought
control be used, it will be found a com-
paratively simple matter to bring down the
blood pressure in the reproductive organs
and send the nervous energy to other parts
of the syſtem and turn it to other uses.

As soon as the sex impulse makes itself
felt, concentrate your attention on the base
of the spine. Attention is directed to the
base of the spine because it is there that the
nerves that control the sex organs have
their origin. Then say to yourself : " The
Divine life force has risen out of my sub-
consciousness and come within reach. I lay
hold of it in the Name of God Who sent it,
and I dedicate it to His service." If the
idea of God does not appeal to you, then
lay hold of this great force in the name of
Humanity, or whatever ideal seems to you
the noblest, but always insist on seeing the
sex force in its highest aspect, see it as it
issues pure and undefiled from its Divine
source ; never try to induce repulsion for
it by thinking of the awful consequences its
illicit uses may bring in their train. If you
were learning to cycle, and you saw a stone
in the road which you wished to avoid, you
would find that if you kept your eyes fixed
on the stone you would hit it with an
accuracy you could never achieve in a
gymkhana, and the more you reminded

yourself of the awful consequences of hitting that ſtone, the more you would wobble out of sheer nervousness. People do not realise the bad effeċts of the wobble of nervousness that is induced by dwelling on the direful consequences of the thing it is desired to avoid. Dwell rather on the good that will be achieved through the thing that it is desired to do ; this reinforces the will with the desires and smooths the path in a wonderful fashion. ALWAYS THINK OF THE THING YOU MEAN TO DO, NOT OF THE THING YOU WISH TO AVOID.

Next visualise the spine as a hollow tube and make a mental piċture of your hand encircling it, and then, with this *imaginary* hand, begin to massage the spine with an upward, squeezing aċtion. Supposing you had a length of soft rubber tubing that had become blocked by some sediment, you could get rid of the obſtruċtion and empty the tube by drawing it through your fiſt, squeezing it as it went, and so pushing the subſtance it contained on ahead of the conſtriċtion in the tube made by the pressure

of your fingers. It is the same process that
you are to use in imagination on the spine,
but you will find it necessary to do it by
repeated pushes, gradually working your way
up the spine with a stroking action, as it were,
for a single imaginary movement will not
impress the picture on the mind sufficiently.

As you perform this process you will
notice a peculiar thing, when working on
the lower part of the spine you will find
considerable difficulty in doing what you
are trying to do, but as you work up the
length of the column the resistance grows
less, and by the time you have reached the
shoulder-level, the invisible energy which
you are to imagine yourself as squeezing up
the spinal column will have begun to flow of
its own accord instead of having to be driven.

As soon as it enters the brain it must be
directed to the intellectual centres in the
forehead, and you must picture yourself as
having a third eye in the centre of the forehead, like the giants of old, and with that
third eye you must imagine yourself to be
looking out on the world from a great

altitude, as if from an aeroplane, so that you see it with a bird's-eye view, remote from yourself. Next you muſt choose some philanthropic movement that is of national service ; you muſt then make a little mental piĉture of the work of that organisation being carried on, and you muſt projeĉt the energy you have dragged up from the base of your spine in a radiant ſtream on to that little mental piĉture, and then imagine yourself to be taking part in the work and *willing* the energy you are sending to be a driving force behind it.

For example, supposing you have chosen the ' Save the Children Fund ' as the special movement into which you wish to pour force, you would make a mental piĉture of one of the food-diſtributing depots (if you do not know what they look like, imagine how you would expeĉt such a depot to appear, accuracy of detail does not matter, you are only using a symbol to assiſt thought), and then piĉture the force from your forehead pouring in a golden ſtream on to that depot ; next imagine yourself coming out of the door of the building with a basket of food on your arm, and distributing it amongst the starving children in their pitiful homes, and the lust that has been in you will be transformed into love and compassion for those children. You could then imagine to yourself their joy and relief, and dwell on this imaginary picture until you began to find yourself feeling pleasure in their gratitude, for as soon as you can induce in yourself an emotion of the higher type, the sensation of the lower type will disappear.

You can apply this idea to any movement which evokes your sympathy, but you must never send this force on to an individual because we know too little of the power of the mind to be able to say what the result would be ; also remember this, that it is not a method that can safely be used for any form of mental healing.

Whether the virtue of this system lies in distracting the attention from the sex sensations, as one distracts the attention of a crying child so that the tears stop, or whether an actual energy goes forth, we cannot say, but at least no harm can be done, and if there is a spiritual power behind the imaginary radiance thus projected, as I like to believe there is, so much the better. Whether the day will come when science shall invent instruments that can prove the projection of a distinct force, I do not know ; experiments have been made with such instruments, but their findings have not yet met with acceptance by orthodox scientists, but any one who tries the experiment I have outlined will soon be under the impression that some force is being sent forth. Whether it reaches its aim or not, cannot be said, but it certainly appears to leave the body.

Now let us consider what would happen if the energy were merely brought to the head and left there, without using the mental picture of social service and projecting it thereon. As a matter of fact, nothing happens ; in a few minutes the sex desires start again with renewed force, whereas, if the mental image of projection be used,

their force seems to be more or less got rid
of. If the desires start again, it is with
much less keenness, and the repetition of
the process two or three times will see the
end of them for the time being. In due
course the impulses will arise again in the
cyclic activity of overflowing life, just as
cyclic for a man as for a woman, though
its periodicity is not so well marked, but
they can be dealt with anew in the same
way. If a very active sex life has left the
veins of the productive organs more or less
permanently dilated, it will take a little
time for these to settle down to normal, but
if this system is persevered with, they will
gradually quiet down and come under
control, so that the organs shall sleep until
activity is required of them. Just as the
brain ceases activity and sleeps when its
blood supply is reduced, or races itself into
insomnia when the blood pressure is too
high, so also do the sex organs ; and it is
the sleep, not the death of sex that should
be aimed at when its activities are not
desired.

VII

THE POWER OF THE SUBLIMATED LIFE-FORCES

IN these pages I am venturing a good deal beyond what orthodox psychology is prepared to acknowledge, so I am merely going to explain a method of manipulating the mind which has been found by experience to give certain results, and not involve myself in arguments by trying to explain how these results are obtained. I am now going to put a bold hypothesis before my readers, and advise them to try its effects in practical application.

As I have previously said in these pages, let us conceive of the Divine Life-force as a stream of energy flowing through the channel of each individual organism and turning the wheels of its machinery. On a mill-stream many waterwheels may be erected on different reaches, one may grind corn, and another may run a dynamo, but the same millstream drives them all. Let us then conceive of the Divine Life-force as a single stream which, if it runs through the machinery of the brain, becomes intellectual activity, thinks great thoughts, plans great schemes, paints great pictures ; and if it runs through the machinery of the muscles becomes physical energy, and if through the machinery of the reproductive organs becomes sex energy. Let us regard this energy as the manifestation of Divine Life, holy in its origin, sacred in its action, and never let us forget that sex feelings are caused by this Divine energy working through the machinery of reproduction. This is a point that must always be kept clearly in sight when dealing with super-abundant sex.

Dirt has been defined as ' misplaced matter.' The farmer speaks of the loam in his fields as ' nice clean soil,' but his wife calls it ' filthy muck ' if he treads it over her carpets. So it is with sex. The marvel-

lous act which gives life is a sacrament ;
the impulses of dawning love beautify the
face and ennoble the character. First love
is usually much more of the spirit than of
the body, there is nothing impure or unclean in its idealistic fervour although the
desire to be near the beloved will soon
develop into the desire for a closer union.
It is the debasing of this sacred force that
gives a sense of pollution and degradation.
The higher a thing is, the more debasing is
its downfall ; the eating of food is not a
disgusting operation, but if one saw a
packet of sandwiches spread out on an
altar, the incongruity of such an act would
cause a feeling of repulsion. The debase-
ment of sex causes such acute disgust because
one instinctively feels that it has come from
so high a source.

This life-force, in its journey from its
spiritual source, becomes first an idea in the
mind, then a feeling in the emotional nature,
and finally a sensation in the reproductive
organs ; we may observe a similar series of
phases in the course of evolution, reproduc-

tion in the lowest forms of life is merely a mechanical act, then, in the vertebrates feeling comes into it, and finally, in man, thought plays a part ; in the higher types of humanity it is felt to have a spiritual significance as well, and therefore the Churches are asked to bless it. All these aspects are present in each individual. Sex has its sensations, its emotions, and its ideals for each of us.

In the previous chapter the problem of the control of the life-force when it had become sex force was dealt with. In this chapter we will deal with the control of the life-force so that it *does not become* sex force. This is a very important point in the life of any one who is unmarried. If we realise clearly that all energy is one, we shall see that if we use a great deal of energy in one direction, we shall have less available for use in another. It may be pointed out in answer to this proposition that men and women of genius have frequently had exceptionally strong sex passions, but if their lives be studied closely, it will be found that their energies are exceptionally strong in all directions, and their sex life was but in proportion to the rest of their nature.

If a great deal of energy goes through the channels of the lower self, it can only be at the expense of the higher self. Whatever we focus our attention upon tends to develop, and if attention be continually focussed upon physical sensations, the whole of the nature tends to coarsen and become more fleshly, as the face clearly indicates.

Many people try to deflect the sex forces into their career by working very hard in the hope of draining them off from the lower levels. This is a course which is very seldom entirely satisfactory, though it is not generally understood why this should be so, and those whose sex forces have legalised outlet advise their less fortunately placed brothers and sisters to ' work it off ' in the self-satisfied belief that they have propounded a solution of the problem if the recipient of their advice would only make the self-denial necessary to take it. They forget that the problem is a physiological one as well as a moral one.

If it be recollected that it is the self-preservation instinct which prompts us to build up a career, we shall see that it is quite a different type of force which is herein employed to that which creates another life ; in one case it is exclusively self-regarding, or ego-centric, and in the second, the whole tendency is to overflow into another.

It is not enough that an outlet should be found for feelings that would normally be directed towards the mate, we must also take into consideration that these feelings will normally have the love of the child added to them in due course, preventing attention from being exclusively directed towards the mate, and thus over-developing the mating aspect of the reproductive instinct. It is too little realised, even by psychologists, that the home-making instinct and the parental instinct are a part of the reproductive instinct and cannot be separated from it in actual practice, because the other two are the logical outcome of the activity of the first. It is for this reason that in the union, even if legalised, in which parenthood is deliberately avoided, the sex instinct is apt to grow unduly strong, and in unlegalised unions is the principal cause of the speedy break-up, owing to the formation of other ties on the part of the man, which is usually their end.

In choosing a channel for the sublimated sex forces we must therefore pay attention to their parental aspect, and select some activity in which the emotions of compassion and protection can flow out in service. As has already been emphasised in these pages, the life-forces belong to the race, not to the individual, and it is to the race they must be returned, if not through one channel, then through another. If we do not serve the race by making and tending the bodies that carry out the racial life, then we must serve it through social service ; but in any case the tremendous creative energy which urges us to mate must never be divorced from the equally divine compassion which urges us to tend and protect the helpless issue of that mating. If we do not have children of the flesh, we must have children of the spirit, else we shall suffer from sex repression.

It may be asked in this respect, what is a person to do who has to earn a living in some monotonous occupation and for whom no prospect of engagement in any definitely social work opens up? Let him dedicate his attitude, if not his energies, to the service of the community, and let him be on the look out for any chance of service to any living creature which may come his way, and into that chance-flung opportunity for giving a cup of cold water let him pour the unused love-force of his nature.

It is significant that the present disproportion in numbers between men and women, and the delaying of the marriage age for economic reasons, reasons which are all the more pressing during a time of national poverty, such as we are going through in this post-war epoch, force on us either the sublimation of a large proportion of the sex forces of the race, or a welter of promiscuity and contraceptives.

At the time when man was struggling with the beasts for survival as a species, numbers were necessary in order to fill the gaps in the tribal ranks, but when his supremacy was assured, his numbers were no longer depleted by the teeth and claws of his rivals, and he therefore tended to overproduction, the resulting over-population being brought down by epidemics due to overcrowding. But now comes the time in our own age when, epidemics having been got in hand by isolation and sanitation, wars are being caused by the pressure of population becoming too great for the land to hold the race that inhabits it, and which therefore overflows on to the land of some other race.

Concurrently with this we see the great increase in organisation for social service, especially such organisations as are motived by love of God and compassion for man ; the people who carry on these organ-

isations are principally the childless and
unmated, and it is because the unsatisfied
love of these solitary souls overflows into
their work that the organisations run by
voluntary workers are so utterly different
in spirit and atmosphere to those run by a
bureaucracy. The relieving officer and
the Lady Bountiful may both give soup and
flannel, and the official soup may be better
in quality than the amateur product, but
there is no question which the poor prefer,
and the sick will go willingly and thankfully
into the cottage hospital who will struggle
desperately to avoid the infirmary wards of
the local workhouse.

The need at the present time is for
quality, not quantity in the children of the
race, and the social worker who labours to
make better conditions for humanity in
general, or any section thereof, is bearing
the race of the future just as much as the
woman who labours in childbirth.

In primitive types of life the whole of
the creature was involved in the reproduction
process ; nutrition stops while the living

jelly-speck grows a waist and comes in half; but the higher we go in the line of evolution, the smaller becomes the proportion of sex life to the total life. In the highly organised communities of the ant and the bee, large sections of the population never have any sex life at all, but give all their energies to the service of the community, and it looks as if a similar state of affairs were gradually being forced upon the human race. If we all reproduced our kind at the Victorian rate, the standard of life in these islands would have to go down until the poverty diseases came in to readjust the balance ; but now that each child needs so much tendance in order that it may share in all the opportunities that civilisation affords, a great number of potential mothers are being absorbed by child welfare work and education, and the actual mother only does a part of the service which the race gives to each new generation.

Any work which makes for human better-ment and ennoblement contributes to the life of the race, and therefore is a suitable substitute for maternity or paternity. Any work which tends simply to self-aggrandisement keeps the life-forces within the circle of the self and is no solution of the problem of sex repression.

VIII

THE BUILDING OF THE HIGHER SELF

I HAVE tried to make it plain that the sublimated sex forces should not be employed to build the personality, but poured out upon the race, because that is their natural channel of flow, and no other substitute is satisfactory. If they be used within the self, an exaggerated egoism may result. If, however, the life-forces are held steadily to the higher level and not allowed to become sexual, they vitalise the whole personality in a most extraordinary way and give it that peculiar magnetic quality so rarely seen and so noticeable when present. Those who have sublimated the life-forces into the service of the race will have little need to complain of a lonely life ; love will flow to them from all sides and their companionship will be sought by

all because they are radiating something
that is as vitalising as sunlight.

As Coué has very truly pointed out, if
we desire deliberately to build certain
qualities which are not naturally present in
us, we have to find some substitute for
spontaneous interest, and we can best find
it in dwelling for some length of time on
the ideas we wish to implant.   Therefore
if we desire to turn the life-force into a
channel other than the one it would naturally seek, we have to perform definite
mental exercises in order to achieve our
end, and these I will now try to explain.

The following exercise for the building of
the higher self should be performed daily
immediately on waking.   Let the thought
rest for a moment on the animal centres at
the base of the spine and then run swiftly
up the spinal column to the intellectual
centres in the forehead, and say, " I dedicate
my life-forces to the service of God through
the race."   You may then consider whatever quality you feel yourself to be lacking
in, and will the life-force to flow in that

quality and strengthen it so that you may be the better equipped for service.

But supposing you are following one of the creative arts as your profession, is it legitimate that you should use the Divine life-force for the purpose of developing your art ? All creative acts are closely allied to each other, and the fact that you are sending force to the higher self will increase the creative vitality of whatever art or intellectual pursuit you are following ; but if you deliberately send the racial forces to the creative centres of the mind, you must be prepared to use your gifts for the service of the race and not for self alone, otherwise ' the swollen ego ' will be developed in you.

Supposing, for instance, your gift is for music, and you vitalised it by the method described in these pages, you would have to be prepared, in addition to concert-giving in the ordinary course of professional work, to give a considerable proportion of your time to playing for charity, and also, still harder task, to helping and teaching those who cannot afford to pay you, and doing all this without thought of return, whether of advertisement or gratitude, simply as your contribution to racial life. If you did not do this, and so insure that the life-forces shall find expression outside the narrow circle of your personality and its limited ends, you would find that your art was taking on the brilliancy of degeneracy.

Supposing, however, you are one of the rank and file, or even of the stragglers of the army of life, what effect will the sublimation of the life-forces have upon your nature if you have no creative talents that can turn them to use? They will give, first of all, a peculiar sense of poise, and that sense of poise will soon be expressed in the alteration of the carriage of the body. There will also come an increased intellectual alertness and power to penetrate into the nature of things; there will be, in fact, a curious quickening and intensifying of all the higher faculties.

The most marked change, however, will

come in your relationships with other people ;
they may not know what it is that they feel,
but they will speedily become aware of
something, and that something is beſt described as personal magnetism. There is a
curious buoyancy of the spirit which comes
when the life-forces are circulating on the
upper arc, also a freeing of the capacities
of the mind. The sublimation and dedication of the life-forces will give personality to
the moſt commonplace charaćter, dignity
to the clumsieſt figure, and spiritual beauty
to the homelieſt face. " I, if I be lifted up,
will draw all men unto Me," said Our Lord.
The uplifted consciousness draws towards
itself all that is higheſt in every human
heart, and the soul that dedicates its life-
forces to service will have little reason to
complain of loneliness and negleċt.

This does not mean that anyone needs to
give up ordinary wage-earning for philanthropic work, but it *does* mean that a new
spirit muſt come into the life, and that some
portion of your energy muſt flow out in
making the world a better and happier

place for others, even for those you have never seen, not out of any hope of gain or gratitude, but simply in order that there may be more happiness in the world.

IX

THE CELIBATE LIFE

WITH the exception of certain primitive cults, all the great religions counsel celibacy as the highest ideal of the life that is dedicated to God ; in considering the problem of the sublimated life-forces, we therefore need to consider the question of the ideal that prompts to celibacy as well as considerations of expediency and force of circumstances which are the more common motives.

I think, however, that there is often some misconception as to what celibacy consists of. I can never feel that a refusal to give expression to burning sex desires is a true celibacy. " Whoso looketh on a woman to lust after her has already committed adultery with her in his heart." Sensitive people are very conscious of the desires that are

directed towards them, even if these desires
find no expression in word or action. To
my mind, the true, dedicated celibacy is
due to a love of God so strong that all lesser
loves are absorbed by it and forgotten. I
cannot believe that God is especially pleased
by the sacrifice of the instincts He has
implanted in us, for they are not evil in
themselves ; but the ties of the householder
take time, and if a man desires to give
himself wholly to the service of God, he
grudges the time demanded by the discharge of mundane duties, however legitimate those duties may be for those upon
whom they are laid, therefore he does not
assume them, and as he is without family
ties, he naturally tends to communal life
with those like-minded to himself, and
that life, being designed to give freedom
from worldly cares, will naturally be of
the simplest description, and so we get
the sisterhood and the clergy-house as the
natural outcome of an absorbing pre-
occupation with the things of the Kingdom,
whether these be regarded from the aspect

of devotion to God or service of humanity.
The principle of religious celibacy is an
absorbing love of God, not the impurity
of sex.

Sometimes, however, the urge of instinct
and the physical habits of generations
persist in the flesh of those who desire to
give themselves to God, and then the
method I have described will be found very
useful in the management of Brother Ass,
especially for those whose work causes them
to deal with the problems of purity in
others, and who therefore cannot keep
their thoughts away from the subject of sex.

There should be no dissociation of the
lower self in those who desire to lead the
higher life, but they should " carry their
manhood up into Godhead " by the process
of sublimation I have described, and effect
a dedication of the life-forces to the chosen
service. Many souls arrive at this method
by experience and intuition, but many do
not, and their attempts to control the
manifestations of sex by the direct use of
the will result in an intensification of these

manifestations because attention is directed towards them, just as the fear of blushing invariably produces a blush. The mechanism is the same in both cases.

In judging the wisdom of the choice of a celibate life we need to examine the motives that prompt it. Many are called but few are chosen, and not every dedication that is offered to God is accepted ; we need to be sure that it is not a pathology based on shock causing sex repulsion which prompts the choice ; that it is love of God which draws, not disgust with man that repels. In the latter case, the sex problem is insoluble till its roots have been laid bare, and the solution of the inhibiting complex is more likely to lead to an ability and desire to mate than a full dedication.

The complete dedication of the life to God is the highest ideal to which any man or woman can aspire, but it is not everyone who is ready for that dedication or whose character would be acceptable to Perfect Purity. We have got to come very near to God in our everyday life and normal state of consciousness before we are ready for the Divine Union, and for many the discipline of home-making is the training which is best suited to them.

What we need is the clarity of vision and perfect self-control which prevents us from developing obsessions and fixations. To be obsessed with the ideal of purity is not less part of the sex complex than to be obsessed with impurity, for both spring from the same root in the subconscious mind, only the latter is an action and the former a re-action ; if thought dwells constantly on the denial of sex we are just as much sex-obsessed as when it dwells on its gratification. The free-moving pendulum swings smoothly through its arc and returns without pause, it is when it sticks at any point that it stops the clock.

We do not want to dedicate a pathology to God, but an ennobled human life which is both whole and wholesome, with the Divine Life-forces running strongly and freely on the highest spiritual levels. Such a life, being in touch with the Divine Life, knows no sense of incompleteness or lack when celibate. If those upon whom circumstances force celibacy would rise into the higher air of spiritual activity instead of fretting behind the bars, they would find that they had attained an inner fulfilment, and, being in circuit with the universe, they were no longer incomplete.

X

THE SEX LIFE OF THE CHILD

THE psychological doctrines of Freud are a most important contribution to modern thought, as epoch-making in their sphere as was the doctrine of evolution, but like evolution, they are liable to misunderstanding, exaggerations and abuse. Wider experience has forced a retreat from some of the positions which it was believed had been conquered in the first rush of enthusiasm, and though many of the general principles have found acceptance, it is by no manner of means certain that all the deductions made from them will hold good. While experts suspend judgment, it is as well for the layman to be very cautious.

The teaching of the New Psychology concerning the sex life of the child has been very much misunderstood and misapplied.

There is a great divergence of scientific opinion, and the two chief authorities on the subject, Jung and Freud, disagree on important points.

So far as my own observation goes, I think that we make a mistake when we apply the word sexuality to the activities of a young child with the same meaning with which we should apply it to the same activities in an adult. It would be just as misleading if we were to use the word 'whiskers' for the soft down on a child's cheek. True, it will become whiskers in time, but it has not done so yet, and is still down. The child-consciousness contains the seeds which will germinate into sex during adolescence, but these are certainly not 'sex' as the word is ordinarily understood. In abnormal and pathological cases premature development may take place, but in the healthy child the development is in proportion to its years, and it is a great mistake to apply the findings of abnormal psychology to the normal, for we may thereby induce the very condition we wish to guard against.

It is curiosity rather than lust that is the motive in the average child's sex life, and the impulse that prompts it is the urge for adaptation to environment. The curiosity of the average child under the age of puberty is quite remote from any idea of personal gratification. It does not apply to itself the information it receives concerning the mysterious ' ways ' of grown-ups, and the knowledge it has obtained of the possibilities of sensation in its own body do not get associated with its sex knowledge until a much later date. It finds that certain parts of its body are more sensitive than others, and that the sensation is pleasurable, therefore it plays with them, just as it shakes its rattle instead of its woolly ball, because the former gives better results than the latter.

If as a consequence of too much stimulus a premature awakening of activity is induced, then we may get the development of a true masturbation habit, but to regard the universal investigation of a baby's fingers as sexual activity is absurd, it investigates its toes and nose equally impartially ; it would be much more ' marked ' if, in its activities, it deliberately ignored a particular part of its anatomy.

A new-born child is not yet used to its body, and derives interest from all its sensations, and one of its chief interests, after food, is excretion. Freud sees in its interest in food a sexual activity, and most psychologists see a sexual factor in its interest in excretion, but in my opinion we should be nearer the mark if we said that the very young child is interested in bodily sensation *as such ;* it is concerned with its sensory system rather than its reproductive mechanism, and the fact that the genital organs come in for their share of investigation does not necessarily show a pre-occupation with sex on the part of the child ; it is only when they can be shown to come in for more than their fair share of investigation that we can talk about un-desirable activities. The baby's view-point is very different to the adult's, for he has no repressions imposed by education, and we have to look at things from his standpoint, if we are to arrive at the significance of his activities. Many a child is simply puzzled by the line an adult takes with regard to acts which have for him no significance, but which speedily acquire one from the importance which appears to be attached to them by the arbiters of his fate. It is far better to turn a child's attention to other interests than to rivet it on the undesired activity by admonitions.

With the growing complexity of a baby's life, impressions coming from the outside compete for his interest with the sensations of his own body, and earlier avenues of interest, having been explored, are abandoned in favour of more exciting activities, and it is not until the true sex tides, rising at puberty, begin to flow in the original channels, that he realises the significance of those channels, and when this realisation dawns, a very large proportion of children pull themselves together and break bad habits of their own accord, parents and nurses often being ignorant

that these habits ever existed ; such at any
rate is the information I have received from
a number of patients undergoing psycho-
analysis.

The question of co-education is a most
important one in relation to the child's sex
life.   It should be considered from two
points of view, however, for the reactions of
a child from a large family of children,
separated from each other as to age by a
year or two at most, a child of a natural
family, in fact, accustomed to nursery inti-
macies, is quite different to that of the only
child, or child from a family of one sex
only.

A child will accept unthinkingly anything to which it is accustomed, but to take
a child from a sheltered environment and
pitchfork it headlong into a mixed school
with sex teaching *ad lib.* from strangers, is
to give that child a shock.

It is argued that Nature mixes the sexes
in families, and therefore we should do the
same in our institutions, but it is not also
observed that in species with a highly

evolved social life, *Nature separates the adolescents !* The young males are driven out
from the herd until such time as they are
come to their ſtrength and can take and
keep a mate.

In my opinion, the ' nursery intimacy '
of the infant school is a good thing, but I
consider that co-education during the difficult years of puberty is putting a very great
ſtrain on both the educational syſtem and
human nature, and that both sexes can be
given a very much better training if they
are kept apart during the perplexing years
of emotional inſtability.

I am quite aware that this attitude is
rank heresy in the eyes of the exponents of
the New Psychology, but I have often been
amazed of the capacity of the devotees of
that ſtill immature science for not looking
at things they do not want to see.

A very great feature is made in modern
psychology of the Œdipus complex, or
fixation of the child's affeƈtions on the
parent of the opposite sex, and while I am
quite prepared to agree that this fixation

causes a certain type of pathology, I am not prepared to admit its truth for the average healthy child.

In assessing the parents' influence over the child, we must not forget the natural hyper-suggestibility of childhood and the enormous prestige of the parent as the arbiter of fate. The child's affection for the parent of the opposite sex to its own may not be altogether unmotived by the fact that the parent of the same sex is usually the disciplinarian. The father thrashes the boys and the mother spanks the girls, or administers whatever the modern psychological nursery is obliged to rely on as the unavoidable equivalent, if such can be found.

We have yet to see what manner of complex the modern unrepressed child will develop when it meets the pressure of the world as a wage-earner, and finds in ' a week's notice ' the delayed equivalent of the much-needed parental slipper.

XI

SEX ENLIGHTENMENT

THE best method of enlightening a child on sex subjects is another vexed question in modern psychology. That the old-fashioned method of a conspiracy of silence was bad, there can be no question, for it caused the child to live in an unreal world and made the problem of his adaptation to environment much more difficult. Neither sex had an understanding of the sex-life and needs of the other, and had to work out the problem experimentally during the early years of married life, often with disastrous results.

On the other hand it is probable that the reaction to an extreme frankness will also be found to have its drawbacks. Ignorance and fear may have been a poor basis on which to build morality, but if they are eliminated, something muſt be put in their place to safeguard sex from misuse.

The more ignorant we are of the physiology of sex, the more difficult it is for us to deal with it, and the faċt that sex is an unsolved riddle makes life very difficult for those whose upbringing has kept them in ignorance. Even if a person is not likely to marry, it is well for them to underſtand the faċts of life, otherwise they may be living in an unreal world, a ' Fools' Paradise ' that has no relation to reality. We need to ſtudy the processes of reproduċtion juſt as impartially as we ſtudy the processes of digeſtion. If the bare minimum of information be hinted at, certain seċtions revealed to the boy, and certain seċtions to the girl, and the rest ſtill shrouded in myſtery, the real value of enlightenment is loſt.

Sex physiology should be dealt with from the scientific, not from the sentimental aspeċt when it is being imparted. The processes of reproduċtion should be ſtudied without personal reference and without apology ; they should, in fact, be de-emotionalised when they are being taught, and the idealistic and ethical side should be dealt with separately. Sex knowledge is not a thing to be afraid of, but it is a thing to be handled carefully. When sex knowledge is given, it should be adapted to the needs of the recipient. A child should never be deliberately misled, but neither should he be encouraged to look upon sex as a commonplace phenomenon, or embarassing situations may result. From the earliest years a child should be taught to regard the Coming of Life as a sacred mystery. It is impossible to give any adequate idea of the physiology of procreation to a very young child, and in my opinion the best way to deal with questions which may often be idle questions and asked with no glimmering of their significance, is to tell the child the thing he has noticed concerns the Great Mystery of the Coming of Life, and that he will be told all about it when the time comes for him to know about such things, until then, it is a sacred secret.

As soon, however, as children show a definite curiosity regarding sex, as distinguished from a natural interest in the inexplicable behaviour of the family pets, let them be told that if they really desire a knowledge of the sacred secret, it shall be given them, and let the communication of sex knowledge be made a solemn initiation. This will stamp it with the association of sacredness and reverence, from which no subsequent experiences will ever be able entirely to divorce it, and will effectually shield the child from the dangers of ignorance without cheapening the most sacred mystery of life.

To my mind, the forced casualness with which enlightenment is often given, with illustrations from the garden and farmyard, debases and familiarises the whole concept, and makes the love of man and woman appear a very simple and commonplace affair, which it is not. Although our methods of reproduction have a very great many points in common with those of the other vertebrates, it is not those aspects which need emphasising, but rather those which are characteristically human and serve to distinguish us from the animals.

Sex purity is not adequately protected by a veil of ignorance, nor yet by threats of disease and disgrace ; its own inherent mystery and sanctity is its best protection, and if this aspect of it be presented to the child-mind on its first enquiries, the impression will be ineffaceable.

The very young child, up to the dawning of puberty, shows, in my experience, little inclination to associate the idea of reproduction with the possibilities of its own nature. It forms a part of the life of ' grown-ups,' and is too remote to affect himself ; he regards the sensations of his body as having no connection with the mysterious process whereby his father and mother gave him life, and when the idea is presented to him, it makes a profound impression, and the child is awe-struck when he realises the powers that lie hidden within him. There is no more effectual way of keeping children from undesirable practices than to tell them that the organs with which they are playing are the ones that will enable them to be fathers and mothers in the future, and that if they do not treat them with very great care and reverence, they will spoil them.

One of the most effectual ways of impressing older children in the early 'teens at a time when ethical and religious considerations are apt to be looked upon as ' tosh,' is to make them feel the pride of race, an ideal to which they very readily respond at this age, and to show them that they are the inheritors of the greatness of the past and that they must hand on the torch of life undimmed to their successors. Make them realise the powers within them, and they will respond in a most remarkable fashion to the appeal. Tell them that they must treat their bodies with reverence so that a fine and virile race may spring from them, and they will fight their own battles with bad habits far more effectually than any amount of threats and supervision can induce them to do.

I have always found that even quite

small children will take sex very seriously,
and adolescents will respond magnificently
to the ideal of racial responsibility at a time
when religious and ethical appeals will
often leave them cold, or even contemptuous.
The religious life is not a thing which can
be forced into activity, and unless it is
spontaneously active, an appeal to it will
supply no motive.

XII

THE PSYCHOLOGY OF MODESTY

THE significance of modesty is very little understood, and I am not aware of any psychological explanation thereof which appeals to me as satisfactory. Professor Westermarck, in a paper read before the British Society for the Study of Sex Psychology, suggested that the instinct of modesty was implanted in the race by the fact that those engaged in the sex act were for the moment defenceless, and therefore found it advisable to conceal themselves from their enemies.

This appears to me to be a most inadequate explanation, and as remote from life as much laboratory psychologising is apt to be. It seems to me that we should recognise two types of modesty, the spontaneous shrinking, and the demureness practised for fear of herd censure for immodesty. A young child is a perfectly blatant creature, but an adolescent is a very shy person. The child in whom sex is undeveloped just doesn't care, and merely defers to the opinions of grown-ups with regard to propriety. He is not modest so much as polite. The person in whom sex forces are developed, however, will lean either to shyness or display ; and the stronger the forces of his nature, the further he will lean in either direction.

The whole issue seems to me to hinge on the question of appetite, whether the individual is in a state of hunger or satiety. When we are hungry the smell of food seems delicious, but after a meal it seems disgusting, and so it is with sex desires.

But in the case of sex we have to remember that there is a very large mental and emotional factor to be considered. A person may be in a state of sex hunger in the abstract, as it were, but when it comes to the actual prospect of satisfying that hunger, a number of æsthetic, emotional and idealistic considerations have to be taken into account. A starving man will not eat grass, and until a person is thoroughly debauched and demoralised he will not look upon any and every specimen of the opposite sex as a possible mate.

We must therefore have an emotional as well as a physical hunger before we are prepared to mate ; and if this complete hunger is not present, we shall be in the state of the person who, after a full meal, smells food and is nauseated thereby. The sex-call will evoke repulsion, and the factor of active repulsion in the absence of desire is, in my opinion, at the root of modesty, for we instinctively avoid arousing sex desire if that attention is not welcome to us.

These considerations do not, of course, apply to a nature that has been debauched, whose modesty is then of the demure type that pays tribute to the *force majeure* of public opinion ; but when the nature is unspoiled, it will tend towards an un-sophisticated display of charms before the one whose admiration is desired, and an inclination to keep quiet or hide in the presence of the bold suitor whose attentions are not welcome.

In fact, the essence of modesty is the avoidance of provocativeness when sex advances are not desired.

It is in this that all customs regarding the avoidance of anything suggestive have their psychological root and all legislation regarding indecency and obscenity its justification. It is not, of course, possible to regulate by law what people shall or shall not do in private, and to attempt to do so by means of legal penalties is to open the way to blackmail, but we can at least see to it that sexual stimuli are not forced on the attention of those who do not wish to be stimulated, and therefore the prohibition of the *public* sale and advertising of pornographic literature, the presentation of objectionable plays and of soliciting in the streets is, in my opinion, most emphatically in the public interest.

Young fellows in the later years of adolescence can be so cleverly wrought upon through the eye and ear that they are no

more master of their own actions than they
would be if they were drunk, and in such
a state they are at the mercy of harpies.

I do not advocate a censorship of publica-
tions or of art exhibitions or private per-
formances of plays, because it is extremely
difficult to say what is artistically justifiable,
and one generation's ' shockers ' are the
next generation's bores, neither should any
limit be set to scientific investigation and
the communication of its results to *bona fide*
students, but the erotic should only be
obtainable by those who definitely set out
with the intention of obtaining it, whether
their motive be good or bad according to
popular standards ; it should not be forced
on the attention of those who do not desire
it. Therefore I advocate the restriction of the
public and indiscriminate proffering of any
form of suggestiveness, and of the advertising of any type of sex interest or any form
of propaganda of immorality, but I do *not*
advocate any legislative attempt to prevent
the private pursuit of such interests, firstly,
because of the difficulty of determining what

is legitimate and what is not, under any
given set of circumstances ; and secondly,
the impossibility of enforcing any such set
of laws without the assistance of the spy
and informer, who are very apt to make
the assistance of justice a by-product of the
chief industry of blackmail.

The immature are already protected from
outrage by the law, and those who have
advances made to them which they do not
desire, have the option of declining or, if
the advances are made forcibly, bringing an
action for assault, in which case the law,
though quite rightly demanding independent
evidence, looks with severity upon the
offender when the case is proved. The
solution of the problem of purity does not
lie so much in the changing of the law in
this respect, as in a more effectual enforce-
ment of the law we already have, and this
is beset by certain difficulties, which would
apply equally to any law that might be
framed. In the first place, it is exceedingly
difficult to get the person who is the victim
of any sexual outrage to prosecute or even

give evidence, because the loss of virginity is so seriously regarded, even if the virginity be loſt through rape, and the victim be entirely innocent of any moral fault. It is only the very public-spirited or the very vindictive who will prosecute under such circumſtances.

The publicity of our courts may have a beneficent effect on the adminiſtration of juſtice and a deterrent effect on certain classes of crimes, but it certainly has the very opposite effect in certain other classes, where the criminal trades on the knowledge that his victim will not face the publicity of a prosecution. The only remedy for such cases is to hear them *in camera*, even if it means depriving some of the Sunday papers of their principal news-items.

Wholesome publicity can be maintained by having a brief report of the proceedings printed with all names and means of identification left out.

XIII

THE PROBLEM OF SELF-ABUSE

SELF-ABUSE may be defined as the artificial production of the reactions of the sex organs, and the whole problem arising out of it wants to be looked at calmly and impartially if it is to be rightly understood and dealt with. Some people hold that self-abuse is a deadly danger, and others that it is entirely innocuous. Speaking from a wide experience of masturbation cases, I am of the opinion that neither concept is a fair statement. The amount of harm done by masturbation depends upon the extent to which it is practised, but though nobody can be at their best either mentally or physically while indulging in this habit, which is a very exhausting one, I have never known it to leave lasting physical effects behind, and recuperation is rapid when it is discontinued. The breaking of the habit of self-abuse is not a difficult matter when its psychology is underſtood.

It has been my invariable experience with regard to those addicted to this habit, and I have dealt with a very large number of cases, that they invariably use phantasy and mental pictures to supply the lack of a partner in their pleasures, and in this phantasy lies the key to the problem of self-abuse, for if it be avoided, the act gives the purely negative satisfaction of physical relief, and soon loses its power and tends to be discontinued.

The actual physical reactions of self-abuse are exactly the same as those of normal intercourse, it is in the mental and emotional aspects that the difference is felt ; and it is because the whole of the higher significance of sex is loſt that its baser aspects are exclusively developed by this practice. As far as the physical evils of self-abuse are concerned, they lie, firſtly in the premature development of sex activity, and the consequent checking of the general growth and development ; and secondly, as do the ill effects of normal intercourse, even in marriage, in overdoing it ; and as the means of satisfaction in self-abuse are always to hand and cost nothing, it is exceedingly likely to be indulged in too freely when once the habit has been acquired.

If a man has a large bank balance, he can afford to spend large sums without overdrawing, but if his income be small, he will soon cripple his resources by prodigal expenditure. The amount of energy that we can afford to express as sex depends on the amount of general energy that is available, and if we expend too much, we shall suffer from exhaustion, be unfit for work, and an easy prey to disease. This applies to married life just as much to irregular unions and self-abuse.

On the other hand, as soon as sexual excess is discontinued, the system speedily recovers, and for this reason some doctors do not hesitate to recommend masturbation as a solution of the sex problem. There is, however, a certain after-effect of self-abuse which has to be reckoned with if it be adopted by adults, and that is the formation of a definite habit of sex reaction, so that none other is possible, and they are unfitted for marriage. This is not so serious in the case of a woman as a man, because she, being the passive partner, can gradually acquire new reaction habits in the course of a few months' experience of normal married life ; whereas a man, being the active partner, if he acquire abnormal reaction habits, will find himself unable to respond to normal stimuli, and therefore unable to play his part, and he cannot acquire new reaction habits by experience, because he is unable to make a beginning. Therefore I consider masturbation a much more serious matter in a man than in a woman. It also in both sexes produces inability to feel sex pleasure if much indulged in, and so is apt to lead to abnormal forms of gratification.

Playing with the genital organs is almost universal in small children, but there is a great difference between a child experimenting with a vague and undeveloped sensation the significance of which it does not realise, and the confirmed adult masturbator on whom this form of gratification has become a fixed habit, rendering normal relations impossible.

A certain amount of self-abuse is exceedingly common in older children and adolescents, and as long as it is not excessive and is not continued into adulthood, it does not seem to leave any after-effects when it has been discontinued. It is a great mistake to try and frighten children out of this habit by telling them of the dreadful diseases it brings ; in the first place, it is not true, and in the second, it fixes thought on the problem to be solved, which is best dealt with by thinking of something else and getting other interests. I have indicated in the chapter on sex enlightenment the line I should take in such cases, and this, together with wise attention to hygiene and regime, and instruction in the sex control methods explained in the earlier chapters, ought to solve the problem. But never on any account threaten a child with permanent disability as the result of his actions, even if it seems likely to result, because the consequent auto-suggestion of fear is most disastrous, and may even lead to hypochondriasis. I should never advise anyone to try self-abuse as a therapeutic measure, although I know it is sometimes recommended even by qualified medical men as a means of transition in the difficult journey from debauchery to continence in cases where the sex problem is a very difficult one. There are medicines which have the effect of lowering the sex pressure, and the use of these is much to be preferred to acquiring the habit of self-abuse, which merely substitutes King Stork for King Log. Such a method is analogous to the use of habit-forming drugs, they may tide over a crisis in an acute illness, but if used regularly, produce a disease of their own. The other alternative more frequently recommended, of resorting to those victims of society, professional prostitutes, is a course as risky to health and reputation as it is abhorrent to decent feeling.

The method of thought-control recommended in these pages, if followed with persistence and common sense, will prove adequate in nine cases out of ten, whether those cases be of a normal sex impulse or of self-abuse. The tenth case, however, requires further help, and recourse should be had to a doctor who specialises in such cases to see whether any physical cause may be at the bottom of the trouble, and under his supervision such treatment can be followed as will probably give great relief and make the problem of acquiring self-control very much easier. In fact, in any case where sexual excesses have produced a neurasthenic or exhausted condition, it is as well to have medical advice, for so much can be done in the way of building up the depleted nervous system and improving the general health. It is much easier to work out the problem of acquiring self-control when the general health is good than when the nerves are all to pieces and insomnia has become an additional problem.

Nevertheless, such physical helps as a good doctor can afford should only be used as a means of tiding over a difficult time ; drugs should not be regular articles of diet, and as the sex problem is with us from adolescence to senility, we ought to learn to manage it by the normal means of self-mastery through thought-control. To have to rely on a bottle of physic to keep us from sin is unmanly.

XIV

ABNORMAL FORMS OF SEXUALITY

WE might define the normal form of sex relationship as that which leads to the procreation of children. This, after all, is Nature's aim, and if we frustrate Nature's aim, we are doing something unnatural.

Abnormal forms of sexuality, or perversions, are not as uncommon as people who have not studied the matter may think, and that is the reason they are referred to in this book. Self-abuse is, of course, an abnormal form of sexuality, and therefore a perversion, but the next most common is homosexuality, which has been greatly on the increase of recent years.

Homosexuality is the production of sex reactions by or upon one of the same sex. There is no need in a book of this nature, intended for the lay reader, to go into the details of any of the perversions ; such information often has the effect of starting people upon the practice against which it warns them, just as Bluebeard's wife could not resist the forbidden room ; it is enough to know that the sex instinct is sometimes subject to deformities so that these, if they be met with, can be recognised and under-stood.

In homosexuality a love is bestowed on one of the same sex such as should normally be given to one of the opposite sex. This love may or may not find physical expres-sion ; not every person with homosexual impulses descends to the practice of un-natural vice ; he or she may, like any other person who loves some one they cannot marry, keep the expression of their feelings within the bounds of propriety, and some of the world's best work, especially in the arts, has been done by people whose feelings could have no natural outlet. It must be clearly realised, if the homosexual is to be understood and helped, that his feelings appear to him to be pure and natural, and that normal love makes no appeal and gives no satisfaction ; he is, however, in the position of a person who is not able to offer marriage to the object of his affections, and to offer love under conditions is dishonourable and can bring nothing but suffering in its train ; and therefore he, like the consumptive, is forced by the nature of his malady to deny himself the gratification of his feelings.

Some schools of psychological thought incline to the opinion that the homosexual represents a third, or Intermediate Sex, and that his view-point ought to be accepted as normal ; but anyone who has studied the subject and seen the effect of unnatural vice on the nervous system cannot fail to see that the whole condition is abnormal and harmful. It is also infectious, for the homosexualist, unlike the masturbator, needs a partner in his pleasures, and therefore is always on the look-out for possible converts, and as the habit of unnatural vice is easily acquired, and once acquired, not so easy to break, it is a serious matter if homosexual propaganda ſtarts in any community. I have seen a wave of unnatural vice go right through a hoſtel for professional women, and many a neurotic can trace the beginning of his troubles back to unfortunate incidents at school. Experienced schoolmaſters know what to look out for, and expulsion follows quickly on detection, but home-keeping women are not so well informed. They need to know that when two people of the same sex play at being husband and wife, indulging in the kissing and cuddling one usually associates with engaged couples, and show the intensity of emotion and jealousy of a passionate love affair, all is not well.

There are two other types of deformity of the love nature which need to be underſtood in order that they may be recognised ; they are not nearly so common as the types we have already considered, but when they occur they cause a great deal of trouble and misunderſtanding because they are very often not underſtood even by the person who is experiencing them. These are known as sadism and masochism, so called after two novelists who made these forms of love the basis of their novels. In sadism, the idea of cruelty is associated with the idea of love, and is the cause of many murders as well as an unnatural violence of temper in married life which is sometimes revealed in divorce court stories. In masochism, however, the idea is to inflict suffering on oneself, and much morbid jealousy has its root in this cause. The psychology of both sadism and masochism is obscure, and their ˙ treatment still more so, but their nature should be understood for two reasons, firstly, because the method of dealing with people who have these abnormal impulses is quite different to that meted out to one who is deliberately wicked. The first intimation a person may have that one of these impulses is present in his nature is to find that he has acted upon it in a moment of emotional excitement, and as realisation dawns, he is bewildered and horrified at his handiwork. A realisation of the nature

of the weakness is often sufficient to prevent
its ever being allowed to get the upper hand
again, and if the injured party realises that
he or she is not dealing with a case of moral
delinquency, but rather with a pathological
impulse of the same type that causes people
to turn giddy and fall off ladders, compassion
will take the place of fear, hate or disgust,
and a soul be saved that would otherwise
be thrust into the outer darkness of social
ostracism.

Secondly, the stories told by those who
are the victims of sadists are so wild that
they are frequently not believed and at-
tributed to hysteria, but it is very difficult
to set a limit to what a real sadist will do ;
and the fact that a man or woman is normal
and kindly in other relations of life is no
evidence in disproof of sadism. Now that
women sit upon juries, they will frequently
have to pass judgment on the handiwork of
a sadist, and they need to understand things
from which they have previously been
sheltered ; it was for this reason that there
arose the better type of opposition to giving

the suffrage and civic rights to women ;
but it is only when men and women co-
operate in dealing with the problems of
sex that they can be solved, and while a
woman's standard of purity makes her stern
in her condemnation of sin, her spirit of
compassion makes her seek to save the
sinner, and while safeguarding society, to
try to heal rather than to punish crime.

XV

WISDOM IN LOVE

IN these days of free social intercourse
between the sexes we need to have a
clear concept of the line of demarcation
which divides friendship from love. To
embark upon a love affair which has no
chance of ending in marriage is to invite
anguish and trouble ; in the old days
parents saw to it that young people did not
compromise themselves with anyone with
whom marriage was undesirable or impossible, but in these days girls, like Becky
Sharp, have ' got to be their own mammas,'
and with ſtrong but unrealised inſtinĉts
urging them on and no knowledge or
experience to aĉt as a break, wisdom is
often bought at the price of suffering, if
nothing worse.

Young people think of love as an emotion

and do not realise that it is a passion until they are in its throes and reason is thrown to the winds. Skylarking and horse-play camouflage what is really courtship, and the barriers of modesty, whose sudden breaking would be resented, get gradually worn away under a progressive familiarity. To a mixture of licence and ignorance add a few cocktails, and the resulting compound is a highly inflammable one.

The entrance of sex feelings into a relationship can always be recognised by two things, the desire to touch, and the desire for exclusive possession. As long as a friendship is free from any impulse to cuddling or jealousy, it is safe and wholesome, but as soon as either of these appear, whoever does not wish to pursue that friendship to the goal of marriage should make their position quite clear, and if necessary break off the friendship before the deeper feelings are involved.

It is a reliable maxim in sex matters that ' if you take the first step, you will take the last,' and once familiarity is allowed to pass the bounds of propriety and the ice of modesty is broken, it is only a matter of time till the plunge is made into the dark waters of the underworld. Passions are stirred and principles thrown to the wind. To play with sex is to play with fire, and the fire that burning safely in its proper place, the domestic hearth, warms the home, may, nay, most certainly will, start a dangerous conflagration if it be kindled in other places. Young people just awakening to adulthood, and having no experience of the dangerous brightness of the consuming flame, have no idea how quickly the pleasant spark of an apparently harmless flirtation may blaze into an uncontrollable fire.

It is a sense of the sanctity of love which is the greatest protection, a feeling that sex is not a thing to be played with, but to be guarded as something sacred. Girls should realise that the male view-point when it comes to love, divides women into two classes, potential wives and potential mistresses, and that they never confuse the two nor transfer a girl from the one to the other

class when once she has been classified.
An honourable man never makes love to a
woman unless he is seeking to win her as
his wife, neither does an honourable woman
encourage attentions unless she is prepared
to consider that man as a possible husband.
As one of the cow-boy characters in that
delightful story, *The Virginian*, said of
the heroine, ' she's square, she don't take
a man's presents unless she means to take
the man.' Such fugitive gifts as sweets, and
flowers and other small tokens are parts of
pleasant social intercourse and need have
no special significance, but if gifts of in-
trinsic value are offered, it should be
realised that they are meant to be ' payment
on account,' and that their acceptance
indicates to the mind of the giver that the
' delivery of the goods ' will be forthcoming.

A man who is wooing a woman for his
wife desires not only her acceptance of him,
but also her family's acceptance of him
and his family's acceptance of her. A man,
on the other hand, who is merely amusing
himself with a girl, is anxious that the affair

should not come to the knowledge of either family. By observing whether a man is secretive or open in his attentions, a woman will be able to form a pretty good opinion as to whether his intentions are honourable or the reverse.

I do not wish it to be thought that I decry the wholesome and helpful comradeship of boy and girl, or man and woman ; that against which I wish to utter a word of warning is the gradual sliding from such a friendship into the intimacy which is the beginning of sex relations ; a possibility which ignorance and innocence does not suspect.

I have been astonished at the extent to which, since the war, educated girls have gone ' week-ending,' believing themselves secure in a knowledge of contraceptives. Did they know as much about these devices as those who did the research work on them, they would feel a little less secure. There is only one thing certain about contraceptives, and that is their uncertainty. A contraceptive has to guard against something that is microscopic, exceedingly active, and exceedingly tenacious of life, and requires very careful technique for its proper use ; and while it reduces the likelihood of conception, never entirely eliminates it. It is reckoned that contraceptives, carefully used, will give a 90 per cent degree of safety, but there is always the remaining 10 per cent to be reckoned with, which is protected by nothing but the god of chance, and the pitcher that goes often enough to the well gets broken in the end. The girl who trusts her reputation to contraceptives will get ' caught out ' sooner or later.

Some ignorant wiseacres think that, as a second string to their bow in case contraceptives fail, they can have recourse to abortion. Now an abortion is the deliberate inducing of a miscarriage, and is severely punishable under the criminal law. It is, of course, the murder of the unborn child, which is a living being from the time of its conception although it has not yet taken up a separate existence. The mother herself runs a greater risk in undergoing an abortion than she does in a normal labour, for at full term, all the tissues that have to separate have undergone certain changes so that they part easily, but when labour is artificially induced these tissues are violently torn apart and parts of them may remain adhering to the wall of the womb, where they die, decompose, and set up blood-poisoning. If through the action of any two people a living soul has set out on its journey through life (even if that soul is unwanted), there is only one thing to be done, according to the laws of both God and man, and that is, to shoulder the responsibility that has been undertaken and do the best that can be done for that child. If the ordeal be well and nobly faced it will go far to redeem the original error. The lapse of time has a wonderful way of solving problems that appear insuperable at the moment, and the worst storms blow themselves out with its passage. The best way to deal with the problem of the illegitimate child is to admit the error and take up the burden. Every one respects

a courageous attempt to make amends for
a wrong that has been done, and more
hands will be held out to help than to throw
stones under such circumstances. There
are many societies that exist for the purpose
of helping in such a difficulty, and the
best person to confide in is the family doctor
or some other qualified medical man in
good standing. He will know the way to
obtain the help that is needed and the best
organisations to go to, for he is used to
having such problems brought to him in
the course of his work, and he is bound to
both secrecy and honourable dealing by
the rules of his profession. The one person
not to go to is the unqualified practitioner,
or the nurse who is willing to break the
rules of her profession and undertake such
a case without a doctor. No reputable
person will risk their professional position
and the life of their patient by doing such
a thing, it is only the sweepings of the
medical or nursing profession that will do
it, and such hands are not safe ones to be
in such a crisis.

When it is realised how wonderful is the mechanism by which life comes into the world, it will also be realised that it is not lightly to be set in motion. It must never be forgotten that even the most normal child-birth causes severe suffering and any abnormality involves grave risk and the intervention of a surgeon. The slightest dirt or contamination causes blood-poisoning ; bleeding often occurs and is sometimes very difficult to stop, and if the labour is prolonged, the heart may give out under the strain. It will therefore be seen what a terrible ordeal a man exposes a woman to when he asks her to risk facing child-birth if he cannot provide her with the care she needs at such a time. True love does not ask it ; the love that makes such demands has its roots in sensuality and selfishness.

I have never yet seen an irregular union which has proved to be permanent. Curious psychological factors come into play in such a union, factors which do not show themselves in the ordinary way of life, and in these lies hidden the beginning of the end.

As soon as a woman yields herself to a man in an unsanctified union, she loses caste in his eyes, and as soon as a man asks this sacrifice of a woman to whom he cannot offer the protection of his name, she feels that his love is selfish and his character contains the elements of weakness. The rift within the lute has appeared, though invisible to the eye, and however the lips may protest to the contrary, the inborn standards of judgment are at work in the subconscious mind.

Finally, there is the problem of the illegitimate child which may be the outcome of such a union ; cast upon the world, homeless, nameless, unprotected, its feet tread a hard path ; the thought of this should stay the hand when all other considerations fail.

What shall be said to the man or woman who has had to learn that evil is evil by experiencing it ? Is it possible for a soul to rise like a phœnix from the ashes of its past, or are there some things which leave an indelible impression upon it ? I have seen a great many men and women who have come up from the depths, and I have always observed that if there is sufficient *COURAGE*, any error can be redeemed. If we make miſtakes, we have, however, to be prepared to pay the price, and if, facing the issue squarely, we shoulder the consequences of our miſtakes and pay off the debt without whining, we can make good, not only in our own eyes and in the sight of God, but of our fellow-men also. The world is kinder than it used to be, and people respeᵭ a courageous attempt to redeem the paſt, however bad it may have been, and many hands are held out to help. Those who point the finger of scorn are beneath contempt, and the ſtones they throw at the soul that is ſtruggling to its feet are generally hurled back at them by the onlookers. The honeſt admission of an error and the fixed determination to make good, command respeᵭ, and as soon as we set out to arise and go to our Father we find that there is a great undercurrent that sets Godward. People may say they do not believe in prayer because when they prayed for a fine day for a picnic, they did not get it, but there are more kinds of prayer than that, and the cry for spiritual help from the soul that admits its mistakes and is fighting to the limit of its strength produces some very surprising results.

The confession of sin as a preliminary to reform is a very deep-rooted instinct of the soul, an instinct which it is sound psychology to obey ; and even in those faiths which do not make systematic use of confession, it is generally possible to find a wise, kindly, and spiritually-minded minister who will help in the bearing of the burden.

But in any case, let us remember that repentance means a turning again, a re-tracing of the steps that have gone astray, not collapsing in an abject heap of misery ; and let us, moreover, distinguish between true repentance, and the self-pity that comes when the inevitable discovery is made that the wages of sin is death. I cannot believe that God likes snivellers, however pious ; but the man or woman

who, however evil has been their life,
ſtands upright, and then walks with un-
flinching feet over the burning coals till
they come back to the ſtraight and narrow
way, has surely redeemed any paſt, however bad. " And when he was yet a great
way off, his Father saw him, and ran to
him." When we set out to go to God, we
meet Him a great deal sooner than we
expeƈt.

The beſt attitude towards an unfortunate
experience is that which Kipling applied
to a disaſtrous war, " We had an im-
perial lesson, It will make us an empire
yet ! "

There is so much more in love than desire
for the beloved, so much more in sex than
physical passion, that an irregular union
can yield no deep and laſting satisfaƈtion.
Unless love can be experienced in its entirety
and beauty, it is better foregone.

Is the path of such a foregoing a sad and
lonely one ? It can be far otherwise. Let
the love be offered up as a voluntary
sacrifice by the lower self to the higher self,

and it will be found to bring not only peace, but power. The magicians of old always invoked their gods with sacrifice, and it is by sacrifice that we invoke the higher powers of the soul ; the love that is caſt aside may bring the bitterness of regret, but the love that is laid upon the altar of noble living brings a light that is all its own.

It is not, however, in the hour of trial, when emotion is at a white heat, that the power to make such a sacrifice can be found ; it does not lie in any ecſtatic emotion, but in the settled habit of the mind, in an integrity which is part of the fibre of the charaĉter. Let each man so live that if he were suddenly called upon as was St. Joseph, to take into his care the Virgin Mother, she might reſt secure in his proteĉtion, undefiled even by thought, and let each woman so live that the nobleſt soul might seek incarnation through her body and come into the world undefiled.